DATE DUE			

12673

630
LAM

Lambert, Mark.

Farming technology.

MESA VERDE MIDDLE SCHOOL
POWAY UNIFIED SCHOOL DISTRICT

TECHNOLOGY IN ACTION

FARMING TECHNOLOGY

Mark Lambert

The Bookwright Press
New York · 1990

Titles in this series

Aircraft Technology

Spacecraft Technology

Car Technology

TV and Video Technology

Farming Technology

Train Technology

Ship Technology

Undersea Technology

First published in the
United States in 1990 by
The Bookwright Press
387 Park Avenue South
New York, NY 10016

First published in 1990
Wayland (Publishers) Ltd
61 Western Road, Hove
East Sussex BN3 1JD, England

©Copyright 1990 Wayland (Publishers) Ltd

Library of Congress Cataloging-in-Publication Data
Lambert, Mark, 1946–
    Farming technology / by Mark Lambert.
      p. cm. — (Technology in action)
    Includes bibliographical references.
    Summary: Discusses machines, breeding, chemicals,
artificial insemination, fertilizers, pesticides, and other
technology employed in modern farming and considers
their effects on our environment and on the future.
    ISBN 0-531-18350-5
    1. Agriculture — Juvenile literature. 2. Agricultural
innovations — Juvenile literature. 3. Agricultural ecology
— Juvenile literature.
[1. Agricultural innovations. 2. Agriculture.] I. Title.
II. Series.
S519.L35 1989   90–30031
630—dc20   CIP
                               AC

Typeset by Direct Image Photosetting Limited,
Sussex, England
Printed in Italy by G. Canale & C.S.p.A., Turin

Front cover The modern tractor is a
technologically sophisticated machine, capable
of producing over 450 hp.

Contents

1 Farming today

The traditional picture of farming is one of peacefully grazing animals, fields of waving grain ripening in the sun and farmers haymaking on hot, sunny days and gathering in the harvest in the late summer and autumn.

Sometimes farming is still like this. However, in recent years a number of major changes have taken place in farming, especially in the developed countries of the world. Modern farming is a business, just like any other. In order to stay in business, farmers have to make a profit. Therefore, they must produce food as efficiently as possible: each ton of grain and pound of meat has to be produced as cheaply as possible.

Farming techniques have changed to ensure efficiency. Some animals still graze in fields, but most are raised intensively in buildings or open pens. There, the animals' environment and intake of food can be controlled more accurately,

ensuring that less food is wasted. Crops are no longer harvested by people equipped with hand tools. Today, there are machines — such as tractors and combine harvesters — that can do the work much more quickly and at a far lower cost.

Machine technology has therefore revolutionized farming and continues to do so. The modern farm is now a place where machines are just as important as crops and animals.

However, not all modern farming involves advanced technology. In many developing countries it is inappropriate, and, in developed countries, the use of technology varies greatly. Arable farms, for example, have benefited greatly from the introduction of machinery, and technology plays a large part in the farming of chickens and pigs. Farming sheep and cattle, on the other hand, involves much less technology. Nevertheless, efforts are constantly being made to make every aspect of farming more efficient, and there is little doubt that technology will play an increasing role in all forms of farming. Farmers have to make sure that these technological advances do not threaten the environment.

Above left In Japan farmers now use machines to help harvest the rice crop.

Below left On a large modern arable farm in one of the world's developed countries, such as the United States, advanced technology is needed to harvest grain crops economically.

Right Sheep, such as these in New Zealand, are generally farmed using very little technology.

The tractor is the most widely used farm machine. It can do a wide variety of tasks. Its introduction revolutionized farming. Five hundred years ago, it took a whole day to plow an acre of land, using oxen. It now takes a tractor pulling a five-furrow plow about half an hour.

The modern tractor developed from steam-powered, stationary traction engines, first used in Europe, the United States and Canada during the 1850s. Soon gasoline engines became available, and engineers began to develop self-propelled machines. The first successful tractor was built in 1889 by the Charter Gas Company in Chicago. In 1898, two American engineers, Charles Hart and Charles Parr, began to produce tractors in large numbers.

The Hart-Parr tractors were enormous; some models weighed around ten tons. The first lightweight tractor was the Ivel, built in England in 1902. It weighed just one and one-half tons. The idea of a light tractor was taken up by the American car manufacturer, Henry Ford, who introduced the first mass-produced tractor – the Fordson Model F – in 1917. Ten years later, Fordsons were being built at the rate of 70,000 a year.

The basic design of the tractor has changed

Henry Ford on one of his early tractors. They had steel tires and the drivers sat exposed to the wind and rain.

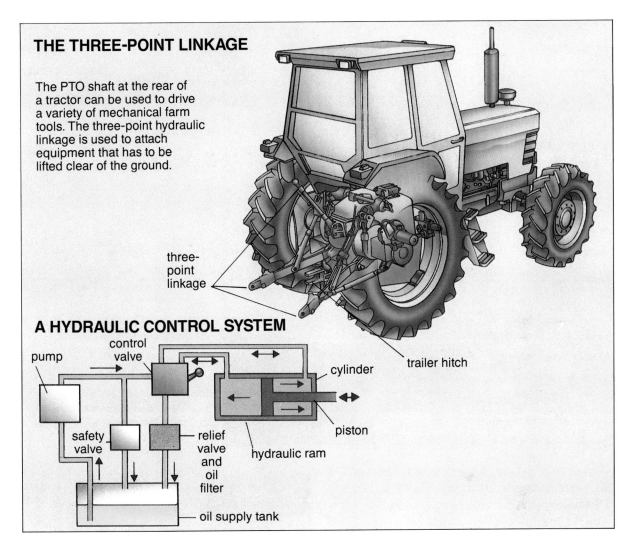

THE THREE-POINT LINKAGE

The PTO shaft at the rear of a tractor can be used to drive a variety of mechanical farm tools. The three-point hydraulic linkage is used to attach equipment that has to be lifted clear of the ground.

three-point linkage

trailer hitch

A HYDRAULIC CONTROL SYSTEM

pump

control valve

cylinder

piston

safety valve

relief valve and oil filter

hydraulic ram

oil supply tank

very little since the early 1900s. Two large rear wheels, equipped with ridges, or lugs, enable the tractor to grip the ground. Two smaller wheels at the front provide steering. The first tractors were fitted with steel tires, which made them very uncomfortable to ride in. Solid rubber tires did not work on such large wheels, but, by the early 1930s, pneumatic (air-filled) tires could be fitted to tractors. Today, a wide variety of tires can be fitted to tractors to suit different conditions. For example, extra-wide tires and ultra-low-pressure tires reduce soil compaction, and narrow tires reduce the damage done to crops.

Early tractors were powered by gasoline engines. However, gasoline was expensive and was soon replaced by a form of kerosene known as tractor vaporizing oil (TVO). Today's more efficient and economical diesel engines were first introduced in the 1950s. A modern tractor engine can deliver an enormous amount of traction, or pulling power, at low speeds. The 1902 Ivel tractor produced just 8 horsepower (hp). The largest tractors now being used are equipped with powerful 8-cylinder, turbocharged engines of over 450 hp.

The first tractors were used simply for pulling trailers, plows and harvesting machinery. However, in 1933 Harry Ferguson, an engineer from Northern Ireland, devised a system of linkages and hydraulic controls (see diagram) that turned the tractor into a much more versatile machine.

7

Left A modern tractor uses hydraulic power to perform a wide variety of heavy tasks on the farm.

Below A modern tractor is equipped with a comfortable cab and controls that are easy to use.

Hydraulic power is used in several ways. At the front of the tractor, it can be used to operate a front-loader. That is a pair of movable arms, which can carry a variety of different tools, such as shovels, spikes and grabs. Hydraulic pipes can be connected to the rear of the tractor to operate such machines as reversible plows and tipping trailers.

Another hydraulic device at the rear, known as the three-point linkage, allows rear-mounted tools – such as plows and harrows – to be raised and lowered. In this way, tools can be carried along when not in use, and the depth at which a plow cuts through the soil can be carefully controlled. The trailer pickup at the rear of the tractor can also be raised and lowered hydraulically.

Fluid pressure is also used in modern steering systems, which makes the steering much lighter. That has made it possible to increase the size of the front wheels in many of today's tractors.

A MODERN TRACTOR

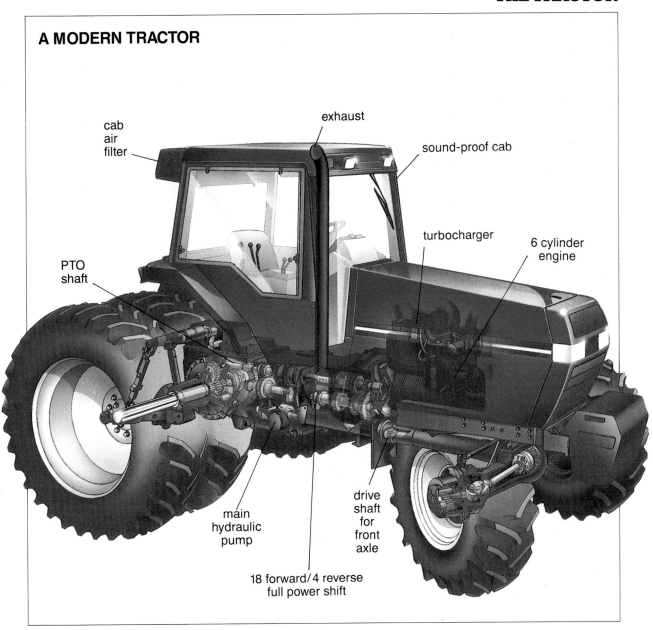

cab
air
filter

exhaust

sound-proof cab

turbocharger

6 cylinder
engine

PTO
shaft

main
hydraulic
pump

drive
shaft
for
front
axle

18 forward/4 reverse
full power shift

The versatility of the tractor is increased by the power take-off (PTO) shaft. This is linked to the engine by gears and is engaged and disengaged hydraulically, to ensure smooth operation. The PTO shaft revolves at speeds of up to 1,000 revolutions per minute (rpm) and is used to power a machine being pulled by the tractor, such as a forage harvester.

The modern tractor is a sophisticated machine compared with the tractors of the early 1900s.

Top-of-the-line tractors now have a four-wheel drive, power-assisted brakes and very light steering. Engine power is delivered to the wheels via a smooth transmission equipped with up to twenty-four gears. Some tractors are fitted with a computer that monitors the performance of all the main working parts. The driver sits in a comfortable, air-conditioned cab, isolated from vibrations in the rest of the tractor by rubber shock absorbers.

The plow was invented over 5,000 years ago. At that time, people had been growing crops for some 4,000 years, but their method of cultivating the soil had been merely to loosen the surface with sticks and hoes. The invention of the plow enabled farmers to break up the soil to a greater depth. This released more soil nutrients and allowed crop plants to grow better roots. Crop yields improved, and people no longer had to move onto uncultivated land because the surface soil of land in use had become exhausted. The invention of the plow meant that fewer people were needed to grow the food required by each community. This left others free to do different tasks.

The first plows evolved from the wooden digging sticks used by the farmers of Mesopotamia. A handle was fitted to the rear of these early plows, and two people dragged the weighted stick through the ground. By 3500 BC, such plows were being pulled by oxen. During the next 3,000 years, farming spread outward from the Middle East, partly as a result of the development of this useful piece of technology.

The main features of the plow as we know it had been developed by about 500 BC. At the front of the plows used at that time, a heavy knife-blade, or colter, cut a path through the soil for the digging blade, or share. Behind the share, a moldboard deflected and turned the turf as it was cut. At that time, farmers in Europe began using iron to protect the working surfaces of plows and make them last longer.

By AD 1000, farmers in Europe were using plows with wheels at the front while some plows

In medieval times a plow was made of iron and wood. Oxen pulled the plow through the ground.

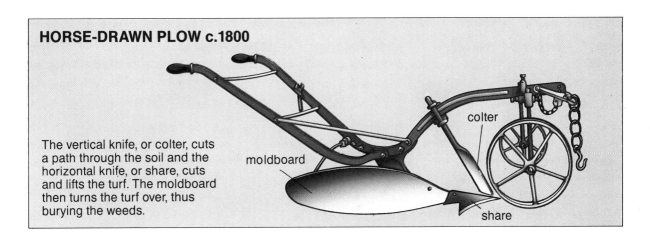

HORSE-DRAWN PLOW c.1800

The vertical knife, or colter, cuts a path through the soil and the horizontal knife, or share, cuts and lifts the turf. The moldboard then turns the turf over, thus burying the weeds.

colter

moldboard

share

had two handles instead of one. Horsedrawn plows began to be used in the eleventh century. The all-iron plow was developed in northern Europe in the late 1700s. In 1789 Robert Ransome, an Englishman, developed a plow with a self-sharpening blade. Ransome's plow was the first to have standardized parts that could easily be replaced if they broke or wore out. In 1837 John Deere, an American blacksmith, devised the first steel plow, in which the bottom (the share and moldboard) was formed from a single piece of metal.

Horse-drawn plows could dig only one or two furrows at a time, whereas modern tractor-drawn plows can plow up to eight furrows at a time. Most have two sets of bottoms, which enable the plow to be used in either direction along a line of furrows. Some plows have bottoms that can be adjusted to alter the width of the furrow. The most powerful tractors can pull a seven-furrow plow and push a five-furrow plow at the same time.

Above By the early 1900s all-steel plows were being pulled by the first tractors.

Right A tractor pulls a five-furrow reversible plow, at the same time as pushing a harrow to break down the soil it has just plowed.

Plowing is only the first stage in preparing the soil for growing a crop. The best crops grow in soil that has been broken down into fine particles. Soils vary widely in their composition and the ease with which they can be broken down. Engineers have therefore developed a wide range of machinery for cultivating soil, and farmers can select the equipment that is most suited to the soil conditions of their land.

One of the oldest cultivation tools is the harrow. Around 300 BC Roman farmers used a spiked frame. A modern harrow is a frame fitted with either spikes or disks, which are set at an angle to the direction of movement. These are drawn over the plowed soil to break down and level the surface. The task can be done more efficiently by using a power harrow. This is a tractor-powered machine that churns up and levels the surface soil using tines, or prongs, set on a rotating drum.

Where a greater depth of fine soil is required, a cultivator is used. The simplest cultivators are unpowered devices with rows of long tines. The tines are mounted on springs so that they vibrate as they move through the soil. A powered cultivator has long, rotating tines that spin through the soil as the machine is pulled forward.

Young plants grow best in firm soil, so before seed is sown, the soil is rolled using a roller. Sowing then takes place, using one of two methods.

A gigantic, four-wheel-drive tractor pulling a harrow. Hydraulic steering makes it possible to have large steering wheels, which in this case are at the rear.

Above The first successful seed drill was devised by Jethro Tull in 1701. The modern seed drill works on the same principle.

Below In a modern pneumatic seed drill, seed is fed from the bottom of the hopper into pipes. Air pumps the seed to the colters, which insert the seed as they cut through the soil.

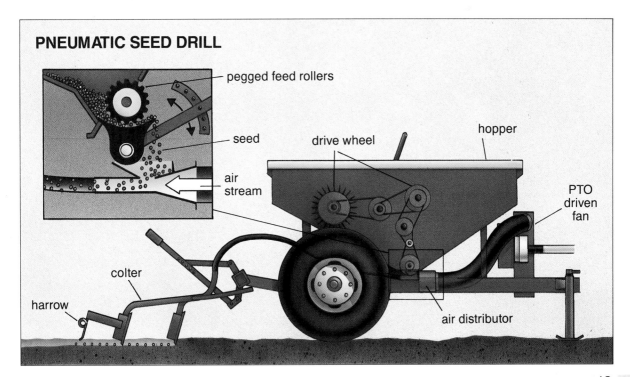

PNEUMATIC SEED DRILL

pegged feed rollers

seed

air stream

drive wheel

hopper

PTO driven fan

colter

harrow

air distributor

Water spraying from a wheeled irrigation system in Colorado.

Grass seed is usually scattered over the surface by a tractor-drawn spreader. The seeds of most other crops are planted by a seed drill, which sows seeds in evenly-spaced rows.

Sowing seeds in rows means that there is less wastage of seed and the young plants are easier to keep free of weeds. The advantages of sowing seeds in rows have been known for thousands of years, but it was not until the 1500s that people began to experiment with seed-drilling machines. The first successful model was devised by Jethro Tull, an English farmer, in 1701. Tull's seed drill cut a small furrow in the surface, dropped the seed in via a tube, and covered it over with soil.

Modern seed drills work in much the same way as Tull's, but technology has improved them. In a pneumatic seed drill, air pressure is used to carry seed from a large hopper to the colters, which plant the seed directly into the ground. Using such drills, large quantities of evenly-spaced seed can be sown in a very short time. Some modern drilling machines also place fertilizer in the ground with the seed. In some cases, a seed drill is combined with a cultivator.

To obtain the greatest possible yield, most crops need to be looked after between sowing and harvesting. Weeds, which compete with the crop plants for food, have to be kept under control. So do pests, such as insects and fungi, that damage the crop plants. A good supply of soil nutrients and water is essential.

Weeds can be controlled by mechanical or chemical means, or a combination of both. Tractor-drawn hoes are used to remove weeds from between the rows of crop plants. Some hoes are combined with machines for spraying herbicides and pesticides. Birds that eat crops can often be kept away by using a gas-powered bird scarer, which produces a loud bang at regular intervals.

Nutrients are supplied in the form of fertilizers, which are generally scattered over the ground by means of tractor-drawn spreaders. In places where the average rainfall is fairly high, lack of water is seldom a problem. In hot, dry regions, however, crops have to be irrigated. This can be done very simply by means of channels or pipes that carry water, either taken from a river or pumped up from a natural store deep underground.

In some places, however, huge, central-pivot irrigators are used. Each consists of a snake-like pipe, up to 1,100 yards (1 km) long, mounted on hundreds of wheeled supports and linked to a central tower. Water sprays out from nozzles along the pipe, and the wheels of each support are driven by an electric motor. The wheels of the outer supports rotate more quickly than those of the inner supports, so that the whole pipe circles around the central tower.

One of the problems of secondary cultivation operations – the tasks that come after plowing – is soil compaction. Every time a tractor passes over the ground, the soil is compressed a little more. This tends to reduce the ability of the soil to produce high crop yields.

To help solve this problem a new machine has recently been devised. It is known as a multi-operation gantry and consists of a frame, 40 or 80 feet (12 or 24 m) wide, suspended between two wheeled modules. On one set of wheels, the engine and driving cab are mounted. The other set of wheels supports a large spray tank. Various implements, such as cultivators, drills, fertilizer-spreaders and sprayers, can be attached to the central frame. As the wheel tracks are so much wider apart than those of a tractor, much less soil becomes compacted.

A multi-operation gantry with the spray boom attachment.

MULTI-OPERATION GANTRY

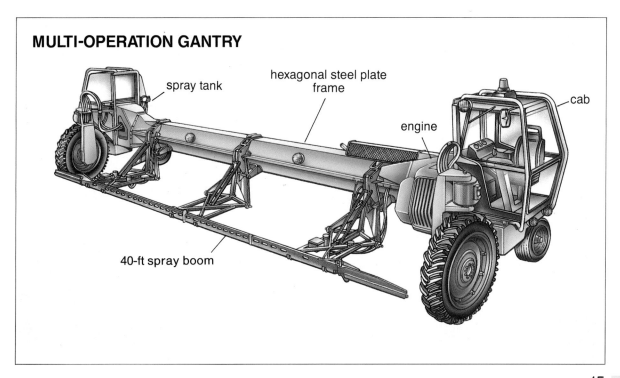

spray tank

hexagonal steel plate frame

cab

engine

40-ft spray boom

Eventually a sown crop is ready for harvesting. In harvesting, as in most farming processes, machines were gradually introduced to perform tasks that were originally done by hand. However, it was a long time before suitable mechanical harvesters were developed. The first threshing machine – for removing the grain of a cereal crop from the straw and chaff – was invented by a Scotsman, Andrew Meikle, in 1768.

Right A combine harvester in the United States, around 1900.

Below A modern combine harvester, in England.

COMBINE HARVESTER

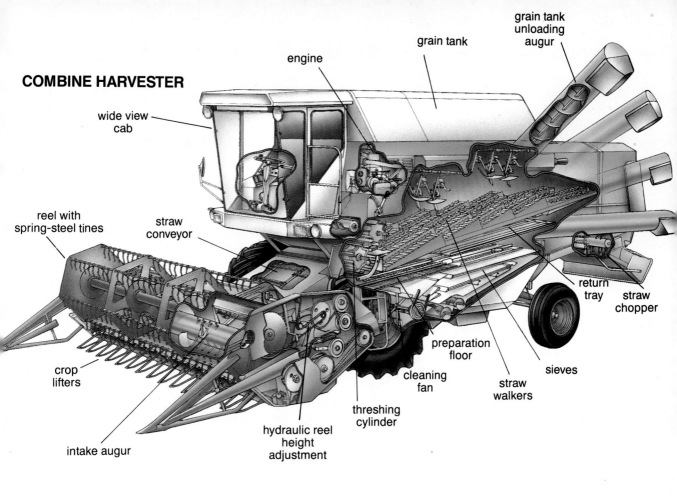

engine

grain tank

grain tank
unloading
augur

wide view
cab

reel with
spring-steel tines

straw
conveyor

grain tank unloading augur

return
tray

straw
chopper

crop
lifters

preparation
floor

sieves

intake augur

hydraulic reel
height
adjustment

cleaning
fan

threshing
cylinder

straw
walkers

Early threshing machines were steam-powered and were generally taken by their owners from farm to farm.

The first machine for reaping grain was invented by the Romans, in Gaul (now France), during the first century AD. However, it only separated the grain heads from the stalks and did not cut the straw. People therefore continued to use sickles until the mid-1800s, when the first machines for cutting grass and cereal crops began to be made.

In the 1830s Hiram Moore and John Haskall, both from the United States, devised a horse-drawn machine that both cut the grain and threshed it. This was the forerunner of later tractor-drawn machines and the highly sophisticated self-propelled machines in use today.

Modern combine harvesters are powered by massive turbo-charged diesel-engines with capacities of over 2 gallons (8l) and power outputs as high as 300 hp. They are designed to harvest huge amounts of grain in a short time. Special leveling devices ensure that they work equally well on flat or sloping ground.

At the front of a combine harvester, a pickup reel draws the grain toward the cutter bar, where the rapidly moving blades slice the stalks off close to the ground. The most advanced of today's machines have a contour-sensing system, operated by ground-pressure sensors, that keeps the cutter bar at just the right height above the ground. The cut stalks, still complete with their heads, are fed by conveyors into the threshing cylinder.

In the threshing cylinder, the grain is rubbed away from the heads, and the awns (bristles) are carefully removed. The straw is carried back to the rear of the machine. The grain falls through sieves and is carried to the cleaning area, where the chaff is removed by a stream of air. The grain falls through more sieves and is finally collected in a storage tank, from which it can be transferred by an auger to a grain trailer.

The driver sits in a comfortable, air-conditioned cab, equipped with a small computer that monitors every part of the machine. Digital displays show such things as engine speed, ground speed and the speed of the various shafts and fans. Warning lights indicate problems, such as loss of speed in any one part, and tell the driver when the grain tank is almost full.

Among the latest harvesting devices now being tried out are grain strippers. A stripper can be attached to the front of a combine harvester in place of the pickup reel and cutter bar. Like the Roman reaping machines used 1,900 years ago, grain strippers remove the heads but leave the straw standing. Using a grain stripper, a field of wheat or rye can be harvested quickly, leaving the straw to be cut when there is more time, or burned.

Cereals such as wheat, barley, oats, rye and rice are not the only crops that have to be harvested. Grass is an equally important crop because huge amounts are used to feed animals in winter. Grass is cut using a mower. Most modern mowers have a set of blades attached to a pair of spinning disks. These cut the grass and leave it in a heap, or swath, behind the mower. The cut grass can then be made into hay or silage.

To make hay, the grass is left to dry in the sun for several days. In ideal haymaking conditions (warm, dry weather), the hay is turned once by a tractor-drawn machine and then picked up and compressed into bales by a baling machine. Three main types of balers are used. One produces small, rectangular bales that are easy for a person to handle. A round baler produces large, cylindrical bales that can be moved only with the aid of a tractor equipped with a front-

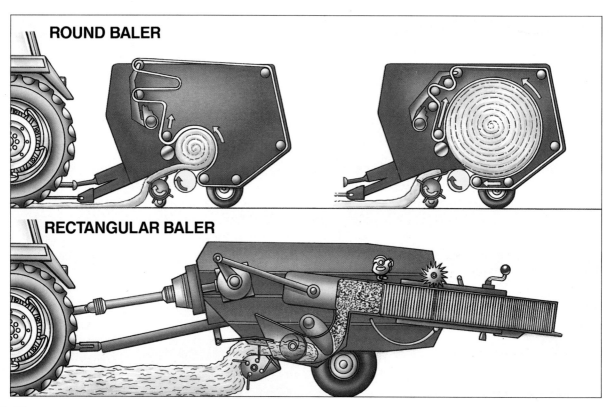

ROUND BALER

RECTANGULAR BALER

Left A self-propelled forage harvester hurls chopped grass into a trailer.

Below A wide variety of produce can now be harvested by machines. Here, a specially designed machine is being used to help harvest pineapples in Hawaii.

loader. The most recently-developed baler produces large, rectangular bales that waste less storage space than round bales.

When making silage, the grass is collected while it still contains moisture. If it is to be stored in a silage clamp or pit, the grass is picked up by a machine called a forage harvester. This is either a tractor-drawn or a self-propelled machine that chops up the grass and hurls it into a specially designed tipping trailer. The grass is then taken to the clamp or pit, heaped up and covered with polyethylene to keep air out. Silage is also made by piling the cut grass into round bales. A tractor-driven wrapping machine is then used to wrap each bale in several layers of black polyethylene.

There are many other crops that have to be harvested. Corn, peas and beans can be harvested using a modified combine harvester. Crops such as apples, strawberries, Brussels sprouts, carrots, potatoes and beets require specially devised harvesting machines.

Agricultural engineers are continually trying to develop machines that will harvest crops more efficiently and with the minimum possible damage to the produce.

Some animals, such as beef cattle and most sheep, are farmed with the aid of nothing more than simple, tractor-powered pieces of equipment. However, other types of animal farming have benefited greatly from the introduction of more advanced technology.

Dairy farming was one of the earliest forms of farming to be mechanized. The first milking machine was devised by Anna Baldwin, a New Jersey farm woman, in 1878. Like all modern milking machines, it worked by suction. However, continuous suction tends to damage the cow's udders. Today's pulsed machines are more like hand-milking or the suckling of a calf, and cause no discomfort to the cow.

Pulsed milking machines were introduced in the early 1900s. A pump creates the necessary suction in the pipes, and a cluster of suction cups is attached to the cow's teats. The milk is sucked into a glass jar, and the yield from each cow can be recorded. It is then pumped to a refrigerated storage tank. The first commercially successful machine was developed in 1918 by a Swede, Carl Gustav de Laval.

For thousands of years cows were milked by hand.

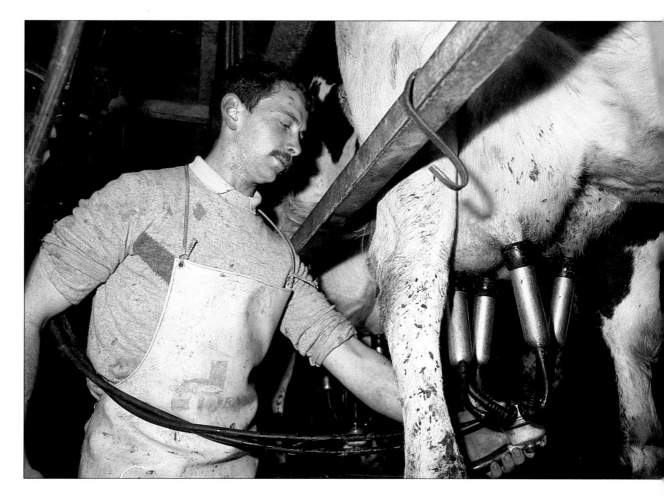

Today, a cluster of suction cups attached to the cow's teats removes the milk.

In cold climates, such as Iowa's, cows spend much of the winter in large, mechanized barns filled with milking equipment. In other areas, where winters are milder, farmers use several types of walk-through milking parlors. The most popular type is the herring-bone parlor, in which the cows stand in two angled rows, on either side of a central passageway. In a 30-cow herring-bone parlor, one person can milk 400 cows in three hours.

The workload can also be reduced by the use of an automatic cluster-remover. This is operated by a combination of suction and mechanical linkages, and removes the milking cluster when an electronic device detects that milk has ceased to flow. In some parlors, computers are used to record information about each cow.

In the most advanced computerized milking systems, each cow wears a collar that carries a radio-signaling device, or transponder. This signal identifies the cow, and when she enters the milking parlor the signal is picked up by a receiver and passed to a computer. The computer's memory stores information on every cow, including calving dates, milk yields and feed requirements. Using this data, the computer instructs a mechanical feeder to produce the right amount of feed and automatically records the quantity of milk that the cow produces. The cluster is removed, the gate is opened automatically and the cow returns to the outside.

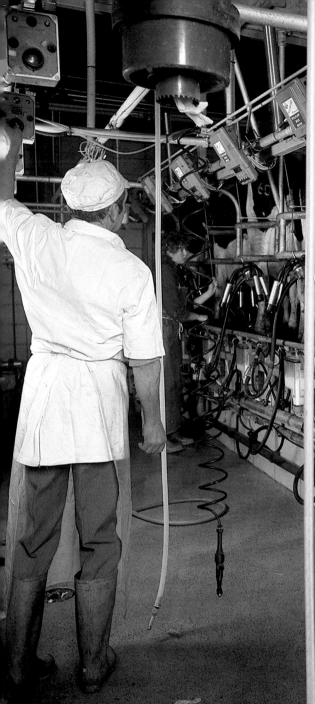
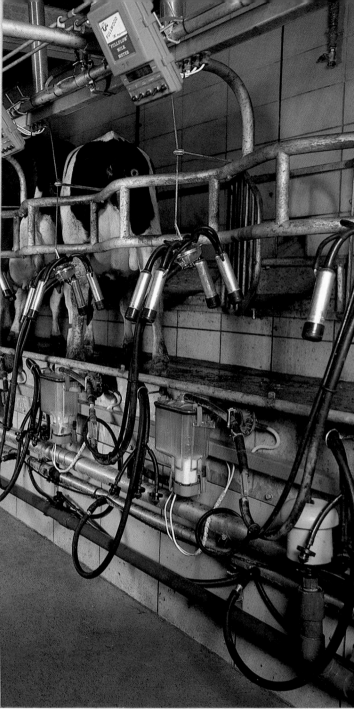

These clusters are removed automatically when the milk stops flowing. Computers measure the amount of milk each cow produces and provide each cow with the right amount of feed at milking time.

The greatest use of technology in agriculture is made on farms where animals are intensively reared indoors. Pigs and chickens, in particular, are often kept under carefully controlled conditions, and technology plays an important part in the farming of these animals.

Pigs are raised for their meat, and it has long been known that they thrive when reared in pens. They do, however, need to be fed in a carefully controlled way. Computer systems can be used to control the amount of food, which is then automatically delivered to a trough, or dropped onto the floor. In one of the latest feeding systems, breeding sows wear radio collars similar to those worn by milking cows and take their food from troughs supplied by a computer-controlled hopper. The computer records every visit that a sow makes to the troughs and allows her to have only a fixed amount of food each day. The advantage of this is that a number of sows can be housed in spacious pens, an arrangement that is thought to reduce stress.

The most automated of today's farming enterprises are those involving chickens. From the first day of its life the environment of a chick is totally controlled. The temperature and humidity of the house in which it is kept are constantly monitored by sensors. These are linked to a computer, which adjusts the ventilation and heating automatically. If anything goes wrong with the heating and ventilation system, a warning signal sounds. The computer can be linked to the telephone system, which enables a warning message to be sent over any distance.

Broiler chickens – reared intensively for meat

– continue their lives in similar environmentally-controlled houses. Weighing machines record the weight of chickens. This enables a computer to calculate the average weight gain of the flock and the amount of food the chickens require. A measured amount of food is automatically delivered from a huge hopper to a trough or pipe in which it is carried along by a chain conveyor. Water is also piped in automatically.

Chickens kept for egg production in battery cages and percheries live in similar conditions. Even the houses used for free-range egg-layers have a considerable degree of environmental control. Manure is removed by automatic machinery, which, in one disposal system, is dried by hot air and thus made easier and more pleasant to deal with. In addition, there are elaborate conveyor systems for the automatic collection and packaging of eggs, some of which can process up to 20,000 eggs every hour.

Conveyor belts are the first stage in an automatic egg-collection system.

Growing plants need nutrients from the soil. They need nitrogen, phosphorus and tiny amounts of other chemical elements such as iron, potassium, sulphur and magnesium. Of these, nitrogen is by far the most important because it is a vital part of plant protein. Plants take up nitrogen in the form of nitrates. These are produced under natural conditions as bacteria break down the chemicals contained in dead plant and animal material, such as animal dung.

By the early 1900s, there were not enough natural sources of nitrogen – such as farmyard manure, potash (from wood burning) and guano (sea-bird droppings) – to meet the increasing demand. The chemical industry therefore began using new processes to produce artificial fertilizers. Today, artificial fertilizers are used in the production of much of the world's food. They contain nitrogen in the form of nitrates, or as compounds of ammonia, which are rapidly converted into nitrates by bacteria in the soil. Such fertilizers release their nutrients more quickly than natural materials and so help plants to grow more rapidly.

Spreading chemical fertilizer. Notice the large tires used in order to reduce soil compaction.

In 1948 the pesticide DDT was used to combat colorado beetles, a serious threat to potato harvests.

There is no chemical difference between the nitrates in artificial fertilizers and those produced by dead organic material. Also, there is no evidence to show that crops produced with the aid of artificial fertilizers differ in quality from crops aided by organic materials. What is certain is that the use of artificial fertilizers has allowed farmers to increase greatly the amount of food they can grow. However, today's fertilizers are products of the chemical processing of crude oil, supplies of which are limited. Many people are questioning whether farmers need to use as much artificial fertilizer as they do. Another serious environmental problem is that excess nitrates are now polluting water supplies in some agricultural areas.

Along with fertilizers, chemical pesticides have dramatically increased food production during the past forty years. Since farming began, weeds, plant-eating insects and parasitic fungi have severely limited crop yields. Today, the chemical industry produces a wide range of chemicals, each designed to deal with one or more of these pests.

The first herbicides that could be used around growing crops appeared in 1932. They were growth-controlling chemicals that killed broad-leaved plants, while leaving cereals and grasses unaffected. By the 1950s, vast amounts of such herbicides were being produced. At the same time, scientists were developing chemicals to deal with insect pests and fungi.

25

Helicopters are often used to spray crops with chemicals such as fungicides.

Some pesticides are produced in the form of liquid sprays; others are in the form of powders that can be dusted over crops. Pesticides are often sprayed by a tractor-mounted sprayer, or a specially designed, self-propelled spraying machine. Sometimes, large areas of crops are sprayed using light aircraft or helicopters.

Unfortunately, being poisonous, most pesticides affect other living things as well as pests. Used carefully, they need not be dangerous to humans. However, they are not always used properly – especially in developing countries – and can endanger wildlife. Also, pesticides and their residues can be present in harvested crops.

Chemicals and drugs are also widely used in animal farming. Farm animals are attacked by a number of parasitic organisms and are regularly treated with drugs that kill such parasites. Many anti-parasitic drugs are given to animals in their feed, while others are designed to be poured directly into their mouths. In some cases, a drug can be poured onto an animal's back, where it is absorbed into the body through the skin.

Animals are also prone to a wide range of bacterial and viral diseases. Where large numbers of animals are kept together, such diseases may spread rapidly, causing suffering to the animals and costing the farmer a great deal of money. Many diseases can now be prevented by vaccines, which – like human vaccines – are generally given by injection or inoculation.

Bacterial diseases can sometimes be treated by using antibiotics. There are two main groups – growth promoters and disease controllers. Certain growth promoters can legally be added to animal feeds. They work by controlling harmful organisms in an animal's gut, helping it to absorb more nutrients from its feed.

Growth-promoting antibiotics have little effect on disease-causing bacteria. These have to be controlled by stronger antibiotics, such as penicillin. The use has to be limited, however, as overdoses can poison animals, and bacteria can develop new strains that are resistant to commonly used antibiotics.

Hormones can also be used as growth promoters. Hormones are chemicals, most of which are produced naturally by glands in the bodies of animals, while several can now be produced by artificial means. When injected into animals, they stimulate certain body processes. However, the use of hormones is very controversial. At present, farmers in the United States are allowed to use them, while they are banned in countries belonging to the European Community. Even so, like certain antibiotics, hormones can still be obtained illegally.

Above Piglets are injected with an iron-containing solution in order to prevent anemia.

Below Australian farm workers administer antibiotics to cattle.

Farmers have been breeding domesticated animals and plants since the earliest days of farming. In nature, a process known as natural selection occurs. This means that organisms with characteristics most suited to their environment are the ones that tend to survive. Early farmers simply copied nature by practicing artificial selection. For breeding they selected animals and plants with the most desirable characteristics. Over thousands of years animals and plants have been selectively bred for such things as size, quality of produce and resistance to disease.

Early farmers had no technology to help them in their selective breeding. They cross-bred their best animals and plants in order to produce new generations with the most desirable characteristics. This process was slow but effective. By the 1800s, selective breeding of both animals and plants had become a fine art.

Sometimes, however, offspring appeared that were very different from their parents; they had undergone a major change, or mutation, during the process of reproduction. In many cases such offspring did not survive, or, if they did, their new characteristics were usually of little or no use. Occasionally, however, a useful characteristic would appear.

The New Leicester, bred in 1760, became the modern Border Leicester.

Above In Israel, cloned avocado shoots of a desirable variety are grafted onto established rootstocks in order to produce fruit within a few years.

Left Cloning plants in the laboratory. Each plant began life as a small group of dividing cells. Each of these cloned seedlings is identical in every respect to the others.

Over the past two centuries, scientists have been learning a great deal more about how animals and plants reproduce. They have also learned more about the nature of mutations. Scientists discovered that chemicals and radiation could be used to cause mutations, and both have been used in the development of several varieties of crop plants, particularly wheat.

The usual way of developing or propagating a new variety of plant is to allow it to flower and produce seed. However, this is a time-consuming process. In some cases, a large number of plants can be grown more rapidly by vegetative propagation, which involves taking cuttings from the original plant. In recent years, however, a more effective method of vegetative propagation has been perfected. Known as cloning, this method involves taking many microscopic fragments of growing tissue from the parent plant and growing them on a nutrient material. Each fragment develops roots and shoots. By using this method, several hundred thousand new plants can be produced from a single parent in a short time.

New breeds of animal are still produced by selective breeding. However, improving stock by normal mating is slow and often expensive. These problems can be partly overcome by transplanting sperm or eggs from one animal to another.

Transplanting sperm is a procedure known as artificial insemination. Sperm-containing semen is removed from top-quality males and stored in freezers. Farmers can breed new stock by having their female animals artificially inseminated by a vet using semen selected from this supply. Artificial insemination enables the characteristics of a top-quality male to be passed on to many more offspring than would be possible by normal mating. This method is used to breed animals such as cattle, pigs and sheep.

The characteristics of top-quality females can be passed on in a similar way. Eggs removed from a female's body can be fertilized in the laboratory, using stored sperm. The resulting embryos are transplanted into the wombs of other females, where they continue to develop.

During the last ten years, some new techniques, popularly known as genetic engineering, have revolutionized plant and animal breeding. A gene is a piece of microscopic material that controls a single characteristic. Genetic engineering involves manipulating and controlling these genes.

In one technique, known as recombinant DNA technology, a single gene is transferred from one organism to another. In this way it is possible to introduce a completely new characteristic into a living organism. This is true genetic engineering.

There are potential dangers in releasing genetically engineered organisms into the environment, and all research is carefully controlled.

Living embryos are implanted into a sheep. Top-quality breeds can sometimes be propagated more easily by this method.

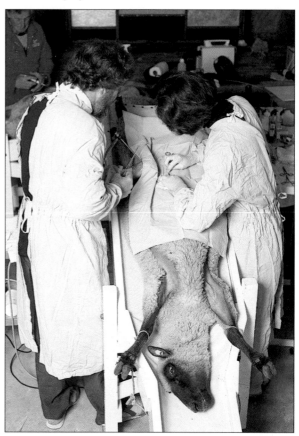

In 1986 strawberry plants on an experimental plot were sprayed with bacteria that had been genetically altered to make them more resistant to frost. The bacteria passed on this frost resistance to the plants.

It will be a long time before animals with genetically engineered characteristics appear on farms. But scientists believe that in a few years they will be able to produce new, improved crop plants. With higher yields and greater resistance to disease, these will reduce the need to use fertilizers and pesticides. In the future, scientists hope to be able to produce cereal crops that can make use of nitrogen gas in the air, the way leguminous plants, such as peas and clover, do now. Crop plants that produce more than one product are also a possibility. Scientists are also trying to develop crops that can be used instead of fossil fuels for energy production.

In modern farmyards cattle produce large amounts of slurry.

The tendency of today's farmers to keep large numbers of animals in relatively small areas has led to a new problem – getting rid of their waste material. This waste can be very useful since it contains large amounts of nitrogen that are good for the soil. However, the waste first has to be broken down, and while this process is occurring, it can cause pollution. Increasingly, farmers are turning to technology to help them deal with this problem.

Basically, there are two kinds of farm waste. When animals are bedded down on straw, their dung and urine mix with the straw to form a manure. This can be spread directly onto the land using a tractor-drawn dung spreader. The tractor's PTO shaft usually drives beaters or flails, which hurl the manure sideways or backward

out of the spreader. (Other dry manures can be spread in the same way and the latest machines can handle up to 12 tons at a time.)

The other kind of waste is dung mixed with large amounts of water. This forms a semi-liquid slurry that is potentially very polluting. If the slurry is washed into watercourses, the bacteria that it contains remove large amounts of oxygen and cause the water to become stagnant. Dung slurries are difficult to handle. In many cases, they are temporarily stored in pits or tanks. There slurries tend to separate into a bottom layer of heavy solids, a watery layer and an upper layer of light solids, which may form a crust. This can be a problem when the slurry has to be moved, but tractor-powered mixing equipment is available. Tractor-powered pumps can be used to transfer the slurry from storage directly onto the land or to other slurry-handling equipment.

A slurry separator can separate the solid material from a large proportion of the water, thus reducing both the quantity of material that has to be disposed of and the chance of pollution. A tractor-drawn slurry tanker can be used to spread the slurry over the land. Alternatively, there are machines that can inject slurry into the ground. This not only reduces the chance of slurry being washed off the land into nearby streams but also cuts down on any smell. Another recently introduced machine is a processor that converts slurry and other wastes into a compost. This can then be spread over the land, or bagged and sold to gardeners.

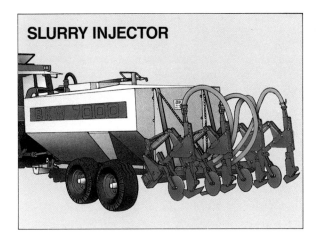

SLURRY INJECTOR

Above By depositing slurry in the ground, a slurry injector reduces the risk of pollution.

A farmer in Bavaria using a mechanical spreader to spread manure over the ground.

Environment and welfare

The increasing use of technology in farming has had many advantages, the chief one being that more food is available at reasonable prices. The spread of technology is inevitable, since farmers have to take advantage of cost-saving technical improvements or else they cannot compete. However, technology has resulted in many other changes.

In many countries, the most obvious changes are to the countryside and the people who live there. Since World War II, governments have encouraged farmers to produce as much food as possible. New machinery has enabled them to turn previously infertile land into productive fields. Also, since machines are easier to operate in large fields, hundreds of miles of hedgerows have been removed to create larger fields.

The population of the countryside has also changed. The increasing use of machinery has meant that fewer people are needed to work on farms. Many country-born people have moved into towns and cities, while at the same time wealthy people from towns have started to move into small country towns. This has changed the nature of village communities. The demand for country houses among people from cities has pushed up property prices to the point where the remaining local people find it difficult to afford houses near their work.

Using modern earth-moving machinery it takes just a few hours to remove a hedge that may have existed for hundreds of years.

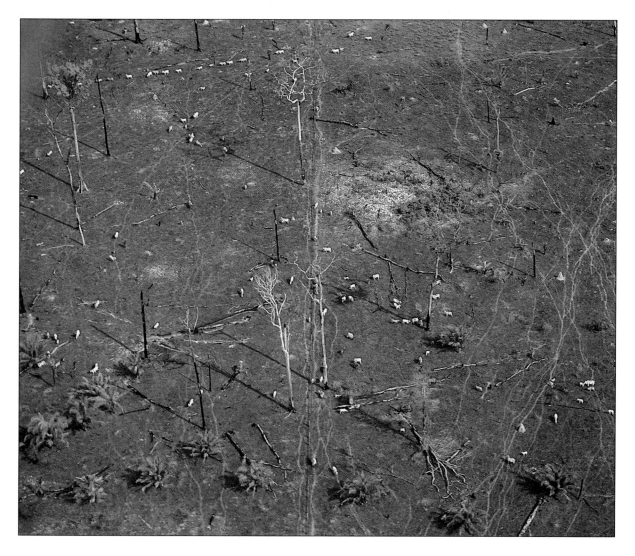

In many parts of the Amazon basin cattle now graze on land that was formerly covered with rainforest.

Farming technology has also had a marked effect upon the environment. Such processes as draining wetland, cutting down woodland and plowing up heathland also remove the wildlife that occupy these habitats. Habitat destruction is now a worldwide problem. In all tropical regions of the world, rainforests are being cut down for lumber or to make room for farming. In Brazil, huge cattle ranches now occupy land that was formerly covered with rainforest.

Agricultural chemicals have also affected the environment. Much of the water in industrialized countries is now polluted by excess nitrates, which are generally thought to come from fertilizers. The nitrates appear to seep down from the surface into the ground water, from which supplies of drinking water are taken. Pesticides also harm many animals and plants, and the numbers of some species have been greatly reduced. One group of pesticides, called organochlorines, is known to be particularly harmful because instead of breaking down, they accumulate in the bodies of animals. They are banned in the United States and throughout Europe, but because they are cheap they are widely used in developing countries.

Some environments have been permanently damaged. Although rainforest soils tend to be poor and unproductive, it has always been possible to cut down a small area of forest, farm the land for a few years, and then leave it for the forest to regrow. However, with modern machines large areas of forest have been cut down, after which the land has been farmed so intensively that the soil has rapidly become exhausted. The land has then been abandoned to weeds and scrub and, in some cases, has been completely eroded by rainwater.

Technology has also contributed, directly or indirectly, to other environmental and social problems. Intensive irrigation of dry lands has in many instances led to a problem known as salinization. This occurs when the salts in the water used for irrigation accumulate in the ground. In many places, salinization has made the soil completely useless.

During the 1960s and 1970s the so-called Green Revolution that took place in many developing countries also created problems. The aim was to grow large quantities of food, using crops such as wheat and corn. However, these crops needed large amounts of chemical fertilizers and pesticides. Many small farmers could not afford these chemicals, and they caused considerable pollution where they were used. These crops also needed a lot of water, and excessive irrigation led to salinization and the spread of waterborne diseases.

Excessive irrigation can lead to salinization — a build-up of salts left behind by the water. This area of land in Pakistan can no longer be farmed.

Guaranteed food prices can lead to food mountains. These French apples are being left to rot.

In some developing nations, crops have been grown on land formerly grazed by herds of domestic animals. These animals have been forced onto more marginal land, which has become over-grazed and desert-like as a result. Combined with other factors, such as drought and war, such conditions can lead to famine.

In developed countries, modern technology has resulted in farming that is much more intensive. This has greatly increased food production, but many people are now questioning the morality of some current methods of farming animals. Chickens and turkeys are often kept in small battery cages or crowded houses. Intensively-raised pigs are also kept in cramped conditions, and in some places veal calves are confined to pens in darkened sheds.

Intensive farming combined with food subsidies often leads to over-production of food. Governments guarantee farmers certain prices for their products in order to ensure that prices will not rise and fall too dramatically. However, the payment systems are often very complex, and sometimes food "mountains" build up. At this point, governments have to introduce other measures, such as limiting the amount each farmer may produce.

In some places farmers are going back to using horses. But it will never again be economically possible to produce all the world's food in this way.

The problems created by today's high-production farming practices have caused some people to consider alternative methods. This does not mean that modern technology is being abandoned. It simply means that some people consider that technology should be used more carefully, and with greater consideration for people and the environment.

In some parts of the world, modern technology is simply inappropriate. Many farmers in developing countries cannot afford complex machinery that can only be operated using expensive fuels. In any case, in such countries human labor is often easily available. It therefore makes sense for farmers to have hand-tools or simple machines that can be operated by people, occasionally assisted by animals. Such tools must be easy to repair. A broken tool is of no use unless a way of mending it is available. Many attempts have been made to improve traditional farming implements. However, people have come to the conclusion that in many places, nothing can yet replace the combination of a simple digging-stick plow and a buffalo. Similarly, traditional methods of irrigation are difficult to improve upon.

In developed countries, modern technology will undoubtedly continue to play a major role. In spite of this, many farmers are now opting for less intensive systems of farming that do not make use of fertilizers and harmful pesticides. Known as organic farming, such systems use natural manures and composts to provide nutrients for crops. All chemical pesticides are excluded, although some natural substances can be used if necessary. Similarly, antibiotics and drugs are not used in the treatment of animals; organic farmers rely on herbal remedies.

Since organic farming is less intensive than chemically-based systems, production is lower. Thus the cost of organically producing food is higher. However, a growing number of consumers are prepared to pay more for food grown

Above An organic farmer plowing growing plant material into the soil as a green manure.

in this way. For the farmer, the process of converting to an organic system can be difficult. It takes two years before fields on which chemicals have been used are considered to be chemical-free, during which time the food produced cannot be labeled as organic.

Below This method of irrigation is cheap, effective and does not use machines that are hard to repair.

It seems likely that the farmers of the future will rely more and more on electronic technology. At present, computers perform relatively simple tasks. They are used for keeping track of accounts and production figures. The computers in today's farm machinery are basically just monitoring devices to help drivers get the best performance from the machines. However, a new generation of computerized farm machines is about to appear.

These new machines will have computers that actually exercise some degree of control. Thus, in a combine harvester, a computer will automatically set the height of the cutter bar and the forward speed of the machine to suit the conditions. At the same time it will monitor such things as the yield and moisture content of the crop. A computer fitted on a tractor will automatically control such things as the depth of a plow and the working speed of a baling machine.

Eventually, some farm machines will be able to operate by themselves, without a driver. Given sufficient sensors and control devices, as well as the right programming, there is no reason

Computer design is increasingly being used to design engines for farm machinery.

Future tractors may look like this model. The engine is mounted beneath the cab. The cab can be turned through 180° and there is a PTO (power take-off) shaft front and back.

why a machine should not find its own way around a field. Robots carrying out such tasks as plowing, harrowing, drilling and harvesting may become a common sight. Even milking cows may be done by robots. At present, it is possible to automate all the stages of milking except placing the clusters on the cows' udders. This is because udders vary a great deal in size and shape. However, farming technologists are trying to develop robot milking-machines.

Meanwhile, there are other problems to be solved. In many developed countries of the world, more food is produced than is consumed. Farmers are now being encouraged to find other appropriate uses for some of their land such as forestry, creating leisure areas and building new houses. Sometimes farmers are paid to leave some or all their land unused for a time.

The opposite problem occurs in those developing countries where agricultural output is low and populations are high. In such places farmers can, in a good year, produce just enough food to feed everyone. However, populations are increasing faster than food production, and if conditions change, as in a war or drought, famine can occur.

There are no easy solutions to these problems. Acceptable ways of limiting population growth

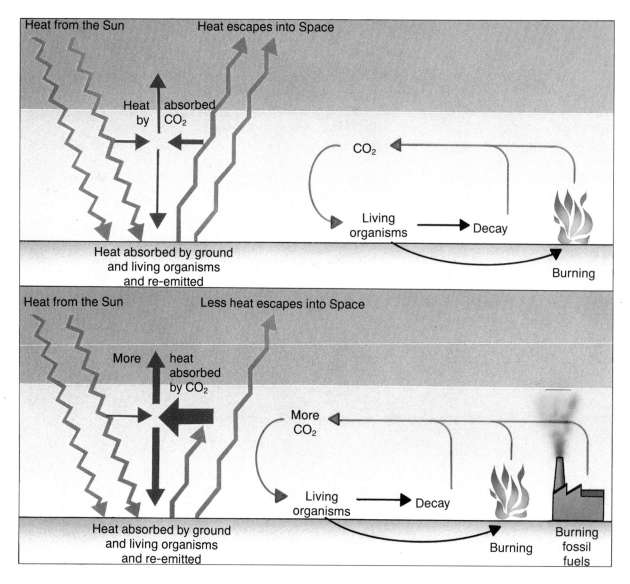

The greenhouse effect. The increased carbon dioxide (CO_2) in the air from burning fossil fuels is causing the Earth's atmosphere to warm up.

are hard to find. If a famine occurs, emergency supplies can be sent from developed countries with surplus food. But this is unsuitable as a long-term solution. One of the aims has to be to encourage the people of such regions to develop farming methods and crops that can be sustained, using cheap and appropriate technology.

If the predictions of some experts are true, measures taken now to organize the way in which the world's food is produced may prove useless within the next sixty years. Many people believe that the process known as the greenhouse effect (see diagram) will result in major changes in the world's climate.

Scientists predict that by the year 2050, the temperature of the atmosphere will have increased by 8.1°F (4.5°C). This will be sufficient to melt large amounts of polar ice, and many areas of land will become flooded with water. Some desert areas, such as the Sahel, might start to receive rain. However, southern Europe and the wheat-growing plains of the central United States will become too hot and dry to grow crops. The wheat areas will move northward into

Canada and northern Europe.

It remains to be seen whether we can control the greenhouse effect by developing technologies that produce less carbon dioxide. On the other hand, it is possible that the world's plant life, both on land and in the oceans, may limit the level of carbon dioxide.

In the distant future there is the prospect of farming in space. Such space farms would be like miniature planet Earths. They would be constructed in space using silica-containing rock from the Moon. Each one would be self-supporting and powered by heat and light from the Sun. Artificial gravity would be created by causing the colony to spin. Water and oxygen would initially be created from lunar dust and, together with carbon dioxide and other wastes, would be continually recycled under a huge plastic dome. Under these conditions, it would be possible to grow only those plants and animals considered to be useful. Weeds, pests and parasites could all be excluded forever.

An artist's impression of a future space colony. The inhabitants will be able to grow their own food.

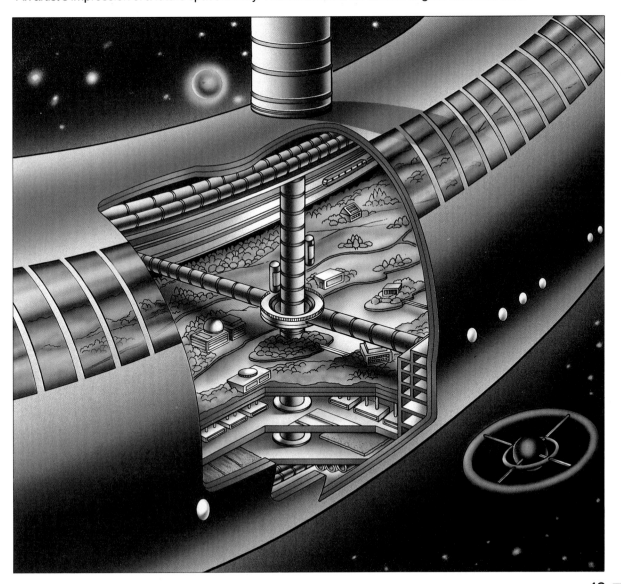

Glossary

Antibiotic Natural or artificially produced drug that is used to treat a bacterial infection.

Arable Fit for cultivation, or plowing.

Auger A device that consists of a spiral column, like a screw, that is free to revolve inside a tube. As the inner column turns, its spiral surface forces any loose material, such as grain or animal feed, up the tube.

Bacteria Microscopic organisms that are neither plant nor animal. Some bacteria cause disease, others are harmless.

Baler A machine used for compressing and tying up hay, silage grass or straw into a compact shape.

Cereal Any cultivated grass that is used to produce grain, for example, wheat and rice.

Chaff The mass of husks that is separated from grain during threshing.

Combine harvester A grain-harvesting machine that combines the tasks of cutting the crop and threshing.

Compost Organic waste material that has been partly broken down by the action of bacteria.

Contour The outline or shape of something; the shape of the land.

Cultivator A machine used for breaking up soil to a depth of 4 inches (10 cm) or more.

DNA Deoxyribonucleic acid. A complex chemical compound that forms the inherited material in nearly every living organism.

Eroded Worn away.

Fertilizer A material used to promote the growth of plants.

Forage harvester A machine used for picking up a crop plant, chopping it up and hurling it into a trailer.

Furrow The groove in the soil made by a plow.

Gene A section of DNA that controls one particular characteristic of a living organism

Genetic engineering The manipulation of genes in the laboratory; in particular, the transfer of a single gene from one organism to another.

Grain The fruit of any grass plant, especially a cereal.

Harrow A device used to break up the surface of the soil into small particles.

Hay Grass that has been cut and allowed to dry in the sun, before being stored as winter feed for farm animals.

Herbicide A chemical designed to kill plants.

Hopper A container, often shaped like a funnel. Grain can be emptied evenly and slowly from the narrow end.

Hydraulic Operated by pressure generated by fluid moving in a pipe.

Intensive farming The rearing of large numbers of animals in an enclosed area for greater efficiency.

Irrigation The process of distributing water to crops growing in dry soil.

Manure Animal dung mixed with another organic material, such as straw.

Marginal land Land that is unusable or unprofitable for farming.

Mower A machine used to cut a crop.

Nutrient A chemical used by a living organism to provide energy or material for growth.

Organic Referring to material that is derived from a living organism.

Pesticide Any poison used to kill insects or weeds.

Propagate To multiply or reproduce.

Radiation The process when certain substances are capable of sending out energy rays, such as alpha, beta or gamma rays.

Residue The chemicals that remain after another chemical, such as a pesticide, has broken down.

Seed drill A machine used for sowing seeds in rows.

Sickle A simple hand tool with a curved blade, used for cutting crops.

Silage Plant material – usually grass or corn – that is stored in a clamp, from which air is excluded. A fermentation process takes place, in which bacteria convert the sugars in the plants into an acid. This preserves the material, including the protein.

Silica A glassy mineral that forms part of rocks such as granite or sandstone. Quartz is a pure form of the mineral.

Slurry A thin mixture of fine solid material in liquid.

Soil compaction The squeezing together of soil particles by pressure from above. This makes it difficult for plant roots to grow through the soil and rainwater to penetrate.

Straw The dry stalks of a cereal crop.

Threshing Removing the grain from the ripe heads of cereal plants by rubbing or beating.

Transmission The part of a motor vehicle that connects the engine with the wheels through a system of cogs.

Turbocharged Powered by a turbine, an engine run by steam, gas, etc., which forces wheels to revolve continuously.

Yield The amount of produce from a given area of land or a given number of plants.

Further reading

America's Farm Crisis by Carol Gorman (Watts, 1987)

The Climate Crisis: Greenhouse Effect and Ozone Layer by John Becklake (Watts, 1989)

Energy by Robin McKie (Watts, 1989)

The Future for the Environment by Mark Lambert (Bookwright, 1986)

Land Ecology by Jennifer Cochrane (Watts, 1987)

Plant Ecology by Jennifer Cochrane (Watts, 1987)

Technology: Science at Work by Robin McKie (Watts, 1984)

Index

Picture Acknowledgments

The author would like to thank the following for their assistance in producing this book: Ford New Holland (Ford of Europe Inc.); CLAAS U.K. Ltd; J.I. Case Europe Ltd.

The publishers would like to thank the following for allowing their photographs to be reproduced in this book: Ann Ronan Picture Library 28; Associated Press 31; Christine Osborne 27 (below); The Ford Motor Company 11 (right), 19 (above); Geoscience Features 12, 34; Holt Studios *cover*, 22, 30; Hutchison 29 (above), 35; Massey Ferguson 8 (left & right), 40; Michael Muldoon 41; Paul Seheult 4 (above), 36; Photri 11 (left), 16 (left); Robert Harding 16 (right); Science Photo Library 29 (below); Topham 6, 25, 37, 39 (above & below); Wayland 5 (Chris Fairclough), 10 (British Museum), 13 (Science Museum), 20, 21, 27 (above), 32; ZEFA 4 (below), 14, 19 (below), 23, 24, 26, 33, 38. Artwork by the Hayward Art Group.